I'm so HUNGRY

I'm so HUNGRY

Sheila Brillhart

ISBN 978-0-557-07081-7

Contents

INTRODUCTION

I am not a nutritionist, dietitian or a doctor. I am an Executive Chef that loves food and suffers from severe asthma. Over 25 million people suffer from asthma; the incidence of the disease has risen in the United States during the past three decades. There is a need for a good cookbook geared towards great healthy food for asthmatics and anyone else that suffers from a chronic disease and uses corticosteroids. Regardless of whether or not there is a specific link between asthma and diet, we do know that we like terrific food, and we know that good nutrition is important for everyone.

My passion for food is profound and exhilarating, and when all is said and done, my work as a chef is about more than food. It's about contentment, satisfaction, and making a connection with others. Being a chef is very personal to me; it allows me the opportunity to live a meaningful and purposeful life, while utilizing my gifts and time on what I feel is a very worthwhile endeavor. Although food is my passion, breathing is my challenge. Most people do not know that food and breathing are connected, and give this concept little thought. My goal as a chef is to increase your understanding of that connection and of the challenges that come with it. I also will convey throughout the book, the importance of clean cooking techniques, and why these techniques relate to your ability to live healthier and breathe easier.

Although no hard scientific proof exists that there is a food-breathing connection, the experts do know that people who eat more antioxidants, omega-3 fatty acids and follow a low-sodium diet have a much better chance of enjoying good health. Antioxidants protect cells from damage, and it makes sense that healthy cells help us breathe easier. Trying to keep all of this in mind presents a special challenge for chefs. That is because, when creating excellent food, the chef's focus must not only be on taste, ingredients, quality, and value, but also on nutrition and health.

Most people take breathing for granted, never even thinking about inhaling and exhaling at all. Most people have no idea what it would be like to struggle for every single breath. Fortunately, there are only a small percentage of us who suffer from such extremely severe asthma. Unfortunately, those of us who have asthma as our constant companion are forced to take massive doses of steroids and get only minimal relief.

Living with severe asthma has taught me how to live with daily discomfort, adjusting to and bouncing back from each asthma attack. It has enabled me to confront each crisis with grace, and to appreciate every day, seeing beauty and opportunity in everything that I do. Living with severe asthma is, for me, like being a good chef: each has helped make me who I am—strong, confident, savoring every day and living my life to the fullest.

Anyone who has ever taken steroids knows that you get HUNGRY and want to eat everything in the house. You also worry about getting FAT. This cookbook will make it easier for you to satisfy your cravings with healthy, delicious foods. When you suffer with asthma or any other disease, there is no downside to eating healthfully and enjoying it.

I love being a professional chef. The satisfaction that comes from preparing a meal and sharing it with others is what I love about my work, and what good food and mealtimes are all about (a good bottle of wine can't hurt, either). Eating delicious food creates warm feelings and fascinating conversation; great memories result from just such occasions. After preparing and serving one of my recipes, I'm positive that one of your guests will attempt to recreate the magic that was so evident when you served that delectable meal to them.

I absolutely love watching people eat the food I have created. I find myself staring and waiting to see their surprise and delight. I absolutely love it when someone takes a bite and closes their eyes as if they has attained nirvana.

My wish for you is that these recipes will radiate the passion and love that it takes to turn whatever ingredients you have on hand into a fine dining experience. In addition, while you are creating this experience, I am certain that you will breathe a little easier and enjoy each moment just a little more. Bon appetite.

Chapter 1: Healthy Coaching

Asthma and Steroids

Most experts agree that very little evidence supports a direct link between food and asthma. However, there is a lot of evidence showing that a well-balanced diet contributes to overall good health and maintaining body weight. It has been suggested that carrying extra weight can put added pressure on the lungs, which leads to asthma-like symptoms.

Steroids - Solu-Medrol: Most asthmatics are very familiar with steroids and the awful side effects that can happen after high doses are given over prolonged periods. The potent effect of steroids can cause the adrenal glands to overproduce cortisol and create a bit of havoc in your body. Some people call this drug "scare-oids." Corticosteroids are drugs closely related to cortisol, a hormone which the adrenal glands naturally produce. Corticosteroids, or glucocorticoids, often just called "steroids," are powerful drugs that can improve asthma symptoms drastically and treat a plethora of other diseases. Steroids are the gold standard for treating asthma attacks and chronic asthma.

Since corticosteroids can fire up the appetite and increase water retention, following a low-salt and/or a potassium-rich diet and watching your caloric intake is advisable. Eat comfort foods with caution: avoid anything greasy, when first starting steroids, as this could aggravate heartburn. In addition, limit sweets and things which are high in sugar content, as steroids will increase blood sugar levels. Also avoid salty foods: These can lead to feeling bloated all over, as well as swollen feet and ankles. Drink lots of water to minimize this effect, which should disappear within a week or so.

Food-Breathing Connection

When we make the connection between what we eat and how we feel, a great change occurs. You do not have to avoid all foods that are high in fat, saturated fat, cholesterol, sugar, and sodium completely. Average intake over a few days, not a single food or even a single meal, that is important to know, however. If you eat a high-fat food or meal, balance the rest of your meals by going with low-fat foods the rest of the day or the next day. Do not beat yourself up over one meal or one food item, and drink lots and lots of water. Yes, you may have a little water retention belly, but that will go away; fat from overeating will not.

Many people who suffer from asthma have "food triggers" that cause asthma attacks. Many things act as triggers, such as allergens or foods that have sulfites. Sulfites occur in foods as a result of fermentation and are found in processed foods such as: beer, wine, hard cider, juice, tea, dried fruits or vegetables (maraschino cherries and guacamole), pickled foods (pickles, peppers and relishes) packaged meats or potatoes (lunchmeats and hash browns). Sulfites also occur naturally in foods like soy products, asparagus, cornstarch, eggs, garlic, maple syrup, salmon, chives, and tomatoes.

Foods with sulfites can make you wheeze; they are a great example of what a food-breathing connection is. Sulfites can make you feel awful; you may not even realize you have consumed something with sulfites, so read all labels. Sulfites are one dietary trigger that is well documented in relation to asthma attacks. The FDA estimates that 1 out of 100 people have sensitivity to the compounds in sulfites. Interestingly enough, people can develop sensitivity to sulfites at any time in life. The cause is unknown. For people who are sensitive to sulfites, a reaction can be mild or life threatening. Seeing an allergist might be helpful to determine if you have an allergy or sensitivity to sulfites.

Side Effects

- **Protect Your Gut**: Steroids causes gastritis and heartburn if taken on an empty stomach. It is a good idea to eat a meal before your medication. Treat yourself to your favorite foods within reason–oddly enough food tastes strange for a couple hours after your steroids. Make sure that you take a heartburn medicine an hour or two before medicine.

- **Insomnia**: Steroids can causes insomnia. Watch out for extra caffeine and sugar during the day. Sometimes warm milk will help you sleep. You need your rest during this time–steroids put a huge strain on your body.

The occurrence of side effects depends on the dose, type of steroid and length of treatment. Some side effects are more serious than others are.

These are some "food-breathing connection" side effects.

- Increased appetite, weight gain
- Acne - sugar, oils
- Diabetes - sugar
- High blood pressure – salt, oils
- Stomach irritation
- Water retention, swelling - salt
- Muscle weakness - salt
- Lower resistance to infection – more antioxidants
- Swollen, "puffy" face and ankles - salt

Remember low-sodium, high potassium diet is recommended, so have a banana a day to keep the doctor away. I should also add that many of the side-effects mentioned last through the "taper" treatment (usually at least six days or so); do not panic if you are still feeling "off." After a few days, you should start feeling better.

Antioxidants

"Antioxidant" is a group name for the vitamins, minerals, carotenoids, and polyphenols that protect the body from harmful free radicals. A high ingestion of antioxidants from fruits and vegetables has been associated with a decrease of adult asthma and other diseases. Several studies have found that asthma in adults was associated with a low dietary intake of fruit and vegetables. Moreover, another study found that asthma occurred less in those with a higher intake of leafy green vegetables, tomatoes and carrots. A similar study at Cornell University linked antioxidants and asthma in children. This study found children with higher levels of beta-carotene, vitamin C and selenium were at least 10 percent less likely to have asthma than those with low levels of these types of antioxidants.

The most well-known antioxidants include the vitamins A, C, E and the mineral selenium found in nuts, meats, tuna and plant foods. Studies have shown the link between free radicals and a number of degenerative diseases associated with aging. Thus, it is possible that antioxidants can be beneficial in reducing the incidence of cancer, cognitive impairment, cardiovascular disease, asthma and immune dysfunction.

To increase your intake of these immune enhancing antioxidants, load up on colorful fruits and vegetables along with leafy green vegetables. Nuts, tuna and other kinds of fish are also great sources of antioxidants.

Super fruits high in antioxidants - berries, blueberries, blackberries, strawberries & raspberries

Vegetables high in antioxidants - kale, spinach, brussels sprouts & broccoli florets

Additional fruits - red grapes, plums & oranges

Clean Cooking

Clean cooking is simple cooking, fresh, light and to the point. Free from dirt, impurities, wholesome and robust, and not comprised of prepared foods. Most clean recipes have few ingredients and are usually very easy to prepare. Fresh ingredients are the most important part of clean cooking.

Cooking techniques are the second most important part of clean cooking. There is nothing like some simple steamed vegetables with whole grain pasta to make you feel great from the inside out. This dish could not be easier to make—and you need little more than a few fresh veggies.

Clean cooking does not mean that you have to become a professional chef or take classes or even invest in expensive knives and cookware. You can use the basic, easy cooking techniques explained in this book to prepare clean foods in healthy ways with everything you already own.

By using healthy cooking techniques, you can cut fat and calories. Consider, for instance, that each tablespoon of regular canola oil you use when frying adds 14 grams of fat and more than 100 calories. To put it in perspective—an adult eating a 1,800-calorie diet should have no more than about 70 grams of fat a day. So we need to cut the fat. By switching to a roasting or grilling technique, you not only eliminate added oil but also allow fat to drip away while maintaining great flavor.

Capture Natural Flavors

This list of cooking methods best captures the flavors and retains flavor and nutrients in foods without adding excessive amounts of fat, salt or sugar. Use them often to prepare clean cooked dishes and capture the natural flavor of foods. These recipes are proven and work. However, you can be creative and make modifications to create even healthier recipes after learning the basics of clean cooking.

Baking, grilling, broiling, poaching, roasting, sautéing and steaming are best methods for clean healthy recipes.

- Use herbs and spices as often as possible; this brings out the natural flavors without adding fats, salts and sugars.

Listen loud and clear: reduce your consumption of fats, especially saturated fat and transfats; you will reduce your risk of many diseases, and may actually breathe a little easier. Eating a low fat diet does not mean sacrificing flavor and taste. It means being smart on how and what you cook with, and watching what you eat.

You can enjoy many of the foods you love with just a few changes. Substitute: yogurt for sour cream or mayo, Splenda or raw sugar for sugar, sea salt for iodized salt and olive oil for canola oil and I Can't Believe It's Not Butter for butter.

Remember, if you are trying to shed pounds or change your diet, calories DO count, so make them count! To lose weight you must burn more calories than you consume even if the pounds are blamed on steroids. Eat more healthy fresh foods with fewer calories.

Low sodium high potassium diets rich in antioxidants are the best combination for many types of diseases. Fruits, vegetables and berries should be eaten in abundance to get that wealth of healthy vitamins! It's recommended to eat 8-10 vegetable servings a day with high levels of antioxidants. You are hungry, so eat lower calorie foods to satisfy your appetite.

Tips

- Watch out for hidden oils and refined sugar, look for sulfites and taste your food BEFORE salting it.

- Portion control! There is no reason to pile food on your plate! Take a reasonable amount of food and you should be good! Or try spreading your meal out into snacks; with this strategy, you will feel like you are eating more.

- Eat slowly. I know when you are hungry eating slowly can be hard to do, but if you take time and chew everything carefully, you are less likely to overeat. Just slow down, and enjoy the food. Sometimes your mouth will actually get tired of chewing.

- If you don't like the food, don't eat it. I know that sounds silly, but we tend to just eat whatever is in front of us. But if you only eat what you really like, that will also cut down on your food intake.

- Use herbs and spices as much as possible when cooking.

- Drink a large glass of water with every meal. Helps fill you up!

- Eat as much fresh food as possible. I know it's tough sometimes, but you must minimize eating packaged food. Packaged foods tend to have much higher amounts of sodium and other bad things for you.

- Keep a packet of gum, lifesavers or tic-tacs around and snack on those when you start craving something sweet, and drink a glass of water.

- Get rid of all the junk. Clean out the refrigerator and fill it with easy quick snacks like carrots, celery, whole fruits, nuts and so on. This will help when you need something to nibble on.

Better Choices for Weight Control

Misconceptions - "Diet" or "reduced fat" foods are not as good as the original version Not always true. Try taste testing and compare; more often then not the healthier choice is the better tasting choice.

The key is making sustainable changes— if you can't live without cookies, trying to eliminate them entirely from your diet won't work. Making the change to a lower calorie, reduced sodium cookie can make a noticeable change in total calories consumed over time.

Cutting soda out of your diet completely can save you 360 calories or more per day. Even diet soda, juices, and whole milk can add calories to your diet. Instead, drink lots of water and switch from whole to skim and from regular soda to diet soda; the little things can make a big difference. Green tea with honey is a great replacement for that soda.

Exercising takes time and keeps you occupied; it will also reduce the amount of food that you will need to cut back on. There are obviously many reasons and opportunities to get moving, so just get up and go.

Listen to your body. Stop eating! If you are full, stop eating! It takes a while for the nutrients in your food to enter your bloodstream, and circulate to the nerve center in your brain that says "stop." Eating slowly is helpful in this regard--you give your body a chance to catch up to your brain and recognize that you have had enough to eat.

Focus on realistic, achievable goals— behavior food modification that you can live with and you like. Small changes make a big difference in your health.

High Potassium - Low Sodium

Potassium - is a mineral salt (electrolyte) essential for maintaining the balance of pH levels in our body fluids. It plays an important role in regulating our blood pressure, bone mass, and many other functions. Low levels of potassium can cause muscle cramps and a whole host of other health problems.

Common high potassium foods: bananas, oranges, apricots, avocado, strawberries, broccoli squash cabbage, tomatoes, potatoes, cucumber, spinach, cauliflower, bell pepper, eggplant, fresh tuna and fresh halibut

Sodium - For low sodium foods, you must read labels and understand what they mean.

Reduced or less sodium:	At least 35percent less sodium than the original
Light in Sodium:	At least 50percent less sodium than the original.
Low Sodium:	At least 140 mg of sodium per serving

Reduce sodium by trying these simple ideas:

Taste your food before salting and try using pepper or lemon juice.

Take it easy on condiments; mustards, catsup, soy sauce, bbq sauce, salad dressings, pre-made sauces and gravies will increase sodium. Look for key words that indicate high sodium content; pickled, smoked, soy sauce, marinated and in broth or in sauce. Most canned foods are high in sodium, replace canned with frozen or fresh when possible.

Whole meats: fresh roasted (broiled or grilled is even better) beef, chicken, fish or turkey are much lower in sodium then pre-packaged lunchmeats. However, a plain meat-type sandwich is lower in sodium than chicken, tuna or egg salad.

FRESH is best!

Do use: spices, herbs, vinegar, lemon, fresh horse radish, baking powder and baking soda for allowed baked products only, low-sodium catsup, low-sodium baking powder, low-sodium baking soda, low sodium sauces.

Don't use: Frozen, canned or pre-made/pre-processed foods.

Healthy Staples

Meats - Whole Chicken, Ground Beef, Roasts, Pork, Sausage and Fish all are great to keep in the freezer.

Eggs - Eggs are possibly the easiest food to cook and can be combined with most any meats or vegetables to create a quick healthy meal.

Low sodium canned goods - Got to haves tomatoes, vegetables, soups and beans.

Canned fishes - Wild salmon, tuna, oysters, and sardines are a great start. These fishes provide protein, omega 3 fatty acids, and calcium from the bones.

Olive Oil and Butter - Of course, no health nut would allow the kitchen to be without olive oil. I use plenty of other cooking fats, like sesame oil, canola blend and butter, but olive oil gets the most use.

Onions and Garlic - I love onions and garlic. Most anything that I cook in the sauté pan starts with a base of sautéed onions and ends with fresh garlic. Caution: always add garlic at the very end or it will become bitter from over cooking.

Fresh Greens - Dark lettuces and spinach are my favorite. Then there are the cooking greens - kale, spinach, chard, collards, mustard greens - that are easy to make as a side dish. They can be steamed, boiled, or sautéed (with onions and garlic) and served along side the entrée.

Tomatoes - Tomato sauce, diced tomatoes, crushed tomatoes and my favorite fire roasted tomatoes all work very well for most anything. Tomatoes are a perfect staple for throwing together a quick meal and have a great gift of lycopene, one of the most powerful natural antioxidant, especially when cooked. Tomatoes have been found to help prevent cancers.

Frozen Vegetables - Frozen vegetables serve a small, but important role in my kitchen. Unbelievably, sometimes I just don't feel like cutting any more vegetables for dinner. There are varieties of blends of mixed vegetable in your freezer department. Just add to broth to make soup or tossed into a skillet with some meat for a meal.

Nuts - Keep nuts on hand like peanuts, almonds, pecans, and cashews. I throw a handful of nuts into my salads and grab a handful while dinner is cooking as a quick snack. Nuts are a great source of good fat and nutrients.

Hint: - Compare foods by looking at prices per pound for best deals and always read labels.

Remember, to plan if using frozen meats from freezer, pulling out of the freezer and refrigerating overnight and is the safest way.

Equipment Needs

Meat Thermometer

9inch baking pan & Round cake pan

Stockpot (just something large enough to boil things in)

Veggie peeler (you can get a lot more uses out of them than you think)

Whisk

Rubber spatula

Heatproof spatula

Wooden spoons

Measuring cups and spoons

8" nonstick sauté, 3qt sauce pan, 5 qt pasta/stock pot.

12" nonstick sauté pan

Sturdy tongs

Box grater

Baking sheet/pan

Mixing bowls

Cutting board

Metal Spatula

Slotted spoon & Soup Ladle

Apron & Towels

Hint: People always ask what knife should I buy? If you cook a lot, spend money on good knives, like Hinkle's... if you do not, buy a stainless steel knife.

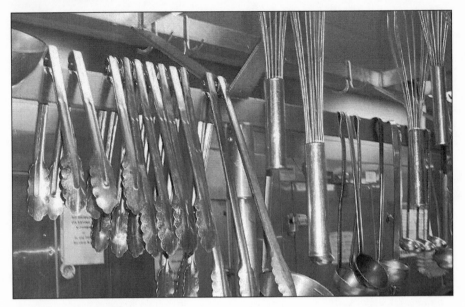

Food Safety

Keep hot foods hot and cold foods cold.

Use FIFO: First In, First Out. In other words, use older product first before you open a newer package.

Label and date leftovers, leftovers should be eaten within three days.

Cover your foods tightly to keep fresh.

Have sufficient airflow around products.

Separate large amounts of leftovers into smaller containers. Cool foods down quickly. *Use shallow pans for cooling large amounts of soups or stews.

Keep your freezer at 0°F. Your refrigerator should be kept at 36–40°F.

Separate stuffing or gravies from cooked products when cooling and freezing.

Freeze fresh meats if you do not plan to cook it within two days after purchase

If not eaten immediately, cooked foods must be kept either hot 140°F to 160°F or cold refrigerated to 40°F or less.

Wrap steaks, chops, and chicken parts separately in freezer bags. Label for ease in selecting. Be sure to press the air out of the package before freezing.

Store uncooked products on the lowest shelf to avoid juices dripping onto other foods causing cross-contamination.

Store uncooked meat/poultry items on same bottom shelf — in separate containers, separate from cooked foods.

Temperature is vital, the temperature range between 40°F and 140°F is considered the "Danger Zone". Food should rest in this temperature range for no more then two hours. Foods sitting more than two hours in this temperature zone should be discarded.

Temperature abuse is the biggest culprit in making people sick. This is when we leave warm food sitting out to long, put it back in the refrigerator, then don't reheat to the proper temperature (160°) when we reheat to eat a second time.

Wash your hands often.

Chapter 2: Let's get cooking

Cooking Methods

Steaming

Steam cooking is an easy and fast way to cook a wide variety of foods, such as vegetables, grains and proteins, while preserving the food's natural flavors. Steam your foods to retain more nutrition and reduce caloric intake you get with other cooking methods.

You can steam vegetables, pork, chicken, eggs, fish and seafood with great success. I don't recommend beef; beef dries up and loses its juiciness.

Here's how it's done:

Place foods in a single layer in the steaming insert, heat liquid to soft boil. This allows all of the pieces of food to have equal exposure to the steam during cooking. Use only a small amount of water when steaming food. For most steam cooking, ½-inch of water on bottom of pan will suffice. Make sure that the water level is at least 1 inch below the bottom of the steaming insert. If the water level is too high, you can just end up boiling your food instead of steaming it. Cover pot and food for about 5 to 8 minutes. Check for doneness. If more time is needed, add more liquid, and check frequently. Food will cook fast, so be careful not to over cook.

Make sure you have a tight fitting lid for your steam pot. The lid helps keep the steam inside the pot for faster cooking. If the lid does not fit properly, or if you take the lid off the steam pot during cooking, steam will escape and the cooking time will increase.

Poaching

Poaching is an incredibly versatile cooking method; just about everything from fruits to meats can be cooked using this technique. Poaching is one of the easiest and healthiest methods of cooking.

To start poaching, the pot should be a bit larger than the fish or vegetables—big enough to cover the meat with about an inch of water or stock. Stock adds instant flavor without calories or sodium. Pick a stock, and add about ¼ cup acid, like lemon juice or vinegar, then add water, herbs or spices. Bring poaching liquid to a boil, then lower heat to a soft simmer. The poaching liquid should completely cover the fish or vegetable by about one inch. This will ensure that the fish or vegetable cooks evenly and will have the proper color and texture when finished. Cooking time varies depending on the size of the fish or vegetable you are cooking. Typically, an eight-ounce portion of fish takes about 10 minutes.

Because eggs cook quickly, the liquid is first brought to a boil and then turned off. Then the eggs are added and covered until cooked to the desired doneness. When poaching eggs, in order to keep the whites intact, it helps to add a bit of vinegar to the water.

Grilling

Grilling is one of the most popular methods of cooking. Whether it's grilled burgers, grilled chicken, grilled vegetables, or grilled salmon, cooking on the barbeque grill is quick and tasty.

Keep it simple; high heat for rare beef (125° to 130°), low heat for well-done beef (145° to 150°). For chicken and pork, cook to 165°, and for fish, anywhere from 125°to 145° When the fish flakes, it is done.

Pre-cook bone-in-chicken in the oven to ensure it's cooked up to 165° without burning. For more delicate foods like fish and vegetables get the grill hot and turn it down once you start cooking.

Something to remember: fat from the food, such as meat, chicken or marinated food, will melt causing the radiated heat from below to rise. The fat or oil will then drop or splash onto the heat source. Upon contact with the heat source, the fat or oil will vaporize or catch fire. This will cause carbon to be deposited (your food may turn black) on the food. To avoid this, turn down the heat or pull the food off until the flame goes out. Despite what some people think, BLACK food is not good-tasting food. DO you want to talk about carcinogens?

Watch your grill when cooking and learn where the hot and cold spots are so foods are placed appropriately.

Roasting

Roasting is a cooking method that uses dry heat. During oven roasting, hot air circulates around the meat, cooking all sides evenly. There are several theories for roasting meats correctly: low temperature cooking, high temperature cooking and a combination of both. Each method can be suitable under the appropriate circumstances.

- A low temperature oven, 200°F to 325°F, is best when cooking with large cuts of meat, turkey and whole chickens that are completely defrosted. The benefit of slow roasting an item is less moisture loss and a more tender product.

- Cooking at high temperatures is beneficial if the cut is small enough (filet, strip loin) to be finished cooking before the juices escape. Do not add water when cooking with high temperature or the meat will dry out, causing an osmosis effect. At higher temperatures, 400° or more, the water inside the muscle is lost at a high rate.

- The combination method uses high heat, just at either the beginning or the end of the cooking process, with most of the cooking at a low temperature. This method produces the golden brown outside and crust people desire but maintains more of the moisture than simply cooking at a high temperature, although the product will not be as moist as low temperature cooking the whole time. Searing the meat then turning down the heat to low before roasting is also beneficial when a dark crust and caramelized flavor is desired for the finished product.

The objective in any case is to retain as much moisture as possible in the finished product, while providing the texture and color people prefer. While roasting meats and vegetables, frequently baste on the surface.

Finishing Roasting Techniques

Leave a thin layer of fat on steaks, chops, and roasts during cooking to seal in juices. Trim fat after cooking. (Fat means natural flavor.) For better browning, pat dry beef steaks, pork chops, and roasts with a paper towel.

Save the juices after roasting. Skim fat off and use drippings and olive oil to make gravy or sauce. If possible refrigerate juice overnight; this gives time for juices to coagulate. A hard fat will collect on top of juices overnight; this should be discarded for a healthier sauce or gravy.

It is very important to roast chicken to the proper temperature to assure safety. Chicken should be cooked until the juices run clear. Check the internal temperature of your chicken using a meat thermometer. Insert the thermometer into the thickest part of the meat, about fifteen seconds. The chicken needs to be at least 165°F. On bone-in chicken, take the temperature next to the bone.

Temperature is vital to all cooking processes.

NOTE: All cooking techniques are exposed to the "Danger Zone" zone. Food should not rest in this temperature range for more then two hours. After that it should be promptly discarded. If you plan on food remaining out in a serving situation for an extended period, be sure to maintain the temperature appropriate to the dish. After two hours at room temperature or in danger zone, toss out. REMEMBER: Keep cold food cold and hot food hot...

Sauté

When you sauté, you cook food on the stove over relatively high heat in a small amount of fat. Usually a shallow pan is used with low sides because that type of pan provides the most surface area. Sauté cooking has a distinct sound, once the oil is hot enough and you add your ingredients you hear the "splash sizzle" sound.

Meats and vegetables are most commonly sautéed. You can use any fat, such as butter (regular or clarified), oils or olive oil. For a healthy oil, blend olive oil and vegetable oil. If you are using regular butter, then it is usually a good idea to add a small amount of vegetable oil to raise the smoke point of the butter. Olive oil has a very low smoke point, so adding a little canola oil facilitates hotter oil without smoking.

The sauté process:

1. Start off with a hot shallow sauté pan such as a non-stick pan, a stainless steel pan or a copper pan. Put the pan on medium-high heat and wait for the pan to heat up.

2. Once the pan is warm/hot, add enough fat to cover the pan, but not any more, about a tablespoon. Let the fats melt and heat up. Remember you are sautéing, NOT frying. Now add the content you wish to sauté. Make sure that all food is evenly cut up. You want uniform pieces in order for the food to cook at the same rate. Keep in mind the ingredients you are using, like carrots; carrots take longer than mushrooms when sautéing. Your food items may take anywhere from 2 minutes to 10 minutes. Taste for preferred doneness. Take stock water or wine and deglaze the pan. To deglaze is to pull up the entire flavor that sticks to the bottom of the pan by

adding a small amount (splash) of liquid to bottom of sauté

3. Don't overcrowd the pan. When you sauté, you want to give the food enough space so it can cook properly. If you overcrowd the pan, there will be too much mass to absorb the heat, resulting in too low heat overall and not enough heat distribution.

4. Stir occasionally (shake the pan) and make sure that nothing burns. Although, if you are sautéing a piece of meat, you might want to give the piece enough time to cook to create a surface area before you stir/turn it.

5. After a few minutes of sautéing over relatively high heat, it's time to lower the heat. How long it takes before you lower the heat depends on what you are sautéing. Broccoli, carrots, cauliflower and potatoes are best if blanched in hot water (partially cooked) before you sauté.

6. Deglaze your pan. After a nice brown coating develops on the bottom of your pan splash in wine, stock or water, this deglazes the pan (takes all goodies off the bottom) and gives the dish more flavor.

Chapter 3: Appetizers

Grilled Chardonnay Shrimp

Ingredients:

16/20 shrimp (medium shrimp)

1 teaspoon red pepper flakes

3 tablespoons sliced green onions

1 tablespoon chopped garlic

4 oz olive oil

3 oz white wine

6 to 8 Skewers

Directions:

Place everything in blender but olive oil and shrimp. Turn blender on low and add oil while blender is running, about 10 seconds.

Place shrimp in glass bowl and pour marination on top. Lightly toss.

Chill for 30 minutes. Grill on open flame grill (BBQ) until pink in color.

Smoked Mac and Cheese

Ingredients:

½ pound elbow macaroni

3 ½ tablespoons butter

3 tablespoons flour mix with 1 tablespoon powdered mustard

3 cups 2% milk

½ cup yellow onion, finely diced

1 bay leaf

½ teaspoon paprika

8 ounces low fat cheddar shredded & 4 ounces smoked gouda shredded

1 ½ teaspoon kosher salt & 1 teaspoon Black pepper

Topping: Optional

3 tablespoons olive oil

1 cup bread crumbs

Directions: Preheat oven to 350° F.

In a large pot of boiling, salted water, cook the pasta to al dente (soft).

While the pasta is cooking, in a separate pot, melt the butter, add onions and cook two minutes. Whisk in the flour and mustard, and keep it moving for about two minutes. Make sure it's free of lumps. Stir in the milk, bay leaf, and paprika. Simmer for five minutes and remove the bay leaf.

Stir in ¾ of the cheese, let melt. Cheese should not stick to whisk when melted. Season with salt and pepper.

Fold the macaroni into the mix and pour into a 2-quart casserole dish. Top with remaining cheese.

Melt the olive oil in a sauté pan, and toss the breadcrumbs to coat. Top the macaroni with the breadcrumbs. Bake for 30 minutes more. Remove from oven and rest for five minutes before serving 4 to 5 servings.

Sheila Brillhart

Chicken Tandoori Quarter Wraps

Ingredients:

½ cup cooked chicken, chopped

4 green onions, sliced

¾ cup plain yogurt

¼ cup tandoori paste

1 tablespoon coriander

½ mango diced

1 tablespoon lime juice

½ teaspoon sugar

1 tablespoon olive oil, for frying pan

Directions:

In a large frying pan, heat oil. Add chicken, tandoori paste, onions and a third of the plain yogurt.

Cook over a medium heat for approx 5 minutes while stirring continuously. When finished cooking cool down to 40°

In a small bowl, combine the remainder of the yogurt with the lime juice, sugar and coriander and mango.

Warm tortilla 30 seconds in microwave, open tortilla wrap, place mix in tortilla, roll up, and slice in two or four slices.

Roasted Red Pepper Hummus

Ingredients:

- 1 can drained chickpeas
- 1 tablespoon tahini
- 1 small can roasted red peppers, drained
- 1 tablespoon lemon juice
- 1 tablespoon chopped garlic
- 1 teaspoon salt and pepper
- 1 teaspoon chili powder
- 1 teaspoon cumin
- 3 tablespoons olive oil

Directions:

Blend all ingredients together in blender but olive oil. Turn blender on low. Add olive oil slowly.

Serve with warm pita bread.

Encrusted tender medallions on croutons

Ingredients:

Filet mignon, about 12 to 14 slices

4 tablespoons olive oil

2 cloves garlic, minced

1 teaspoon rosemary

1 teaspoon thyme

1 teaspoon marjoram

¼ teaspoon salt

¼ teaspoon black

14 thin sliced French bread toasted croutons

¼ cup crumbled blue cheese

Directions:

Heat olive oil and garlic in a covered microwave safe bowl for about 50 to 60 seconds, until hot. Remove and allow cooling. Add herbs and stir. Place filet mignon on a shallow glass dish. Pour herb mixture over and turn steaks to coat. Cover and let marinate for 1 to 3 hours in refrigerator. Preheat grill for high heat. Remove steaks, remove excess oil, and season with salt and pepper. Place on grill and cook for 5-6 minutes. Remove from heat and place on toasted french bread; top with blue cheese melt under broiler.

- Garnish with blue cheese and melt.

Portobello Fries with Horseradish Sauce

Ingredients:

4 large Portobello mushroom caps

Extra-virgin olive oil, for drizzling, plus 1/4 cup vegetable oil

2 tablespoons low sodium steak seasoning blend or coarse salt and black pepper mix

2 eggs, 1/3 skim milk whisk (egg wash) together

1/4 cup flat-leaf parsley, chopped

1-cup bread crumbs

1/2 -cup parmesan.

Sauce: 2 tablespoons prepared low sodium horseradish

1/3 cup light sour cream or 1/3 cup plain yogurt & 1/3 cup light mayo

1-tablespoon lemon juice

1 tablespoon Dijon

Mix together, set aside

Directions:

Preheat broiler.

Scrape the gills off the underside of Portobello mushroom caps with a spoon. Brush caps gently with a damp cloth to clean them. Drizzle caps with oil to keep them from sticking to the broiler pan and season the caps with steak seasoning or salt and black pepper.

Grill mushrooms 3 or 4 minutes on each side under a loose tin foil tent until just tender. Remove from heat and cool 5 minutes.

Slice grilled caps into 1/2-inch strips. Turn strips in egg wash, then coat in mixture of parsley, breadcrumbs and cheese. Cook "fries" over medium high heat in enough oil to coat a nonstick skillet in a thin layer, about 1/4 cup. "Fries" will brown in 2 or 3 minutes on each side. Pull out and pat dry with paper towel.

Tasty Quesadilla

Ingredients:

Mix 1-teaspoon cumin and 1-teaspoon kosher salt

Vegetable oil spray

1 can diced green chili drained

8 ounces sliced fresh mushrooms

½ medium onion, thinly sliced and separated into rings

1 teaspoon minced garlic

3 tablespoons chopped fresh cilantro

3 8-inch whole-wheat flour tortillas or regular tortillas

6 tablespoons shredded low-fat Monterey Jack cheese with jalapeño peppers or low-fat Cheddar cheese

Directions:

Preheat oven to 350°F.

Mix cumin & kosher salt set aside

Spray a large skillet with vegetable oil spray. Cook chili, mushrooms, onion, and garlic in skillet over medium heat until onion is tender, about 5 to 7 minutes...

Arrange one-third of the mushroom mixture on half of one tortilla. Sprinkle with 2 tablespoons of the cheese. Fold the other half of the tortilla over cheese. Place on a baking sheet spray with oil dust with cumin salt mix. Repeat with remaining ingredients to makes 3 quesadillas

Garnish with chopped cilantro.

Bake quesadillas about 5 minutes or until filling is hot and cheese melts.

Cut each quesadilla into four wedges. Serve warm — with salsa, if desired.

Chapter 4: Soups and Sauces

Thickener

Roux

Pour about ¼ c. of the oil in a small sturdy pan and place it over medium-low heat.

- When the oil is warm but not too hot, start stirring in flour until the mixture is thick - about the texture of wet concrete. Add more oil or flour until its right.
- Stir continually with the wooden spoon over the heat so the roux cooks. The flour will gradually begin to brown. The roux can be used when the flour is light golden in color. The darker you cook the roux, the more flavors it will add to the sauce or gravy
- Transfer the roux to another container to cool.
- Store roux in the refrigerator for a week, or freeze it.

Cornstarch slurry

Cornstarch slurry is cold liquid mixed with cornstarch until smooth and glossy.

- This slurry is used to thicken sauces, soups, stews and desserts.
- With twice the thickening power as regular flour, cornstarch is preferred in recipes that call for a thickened clear sauce instead of an opaque sauce.
- Pour cornstarch in a bowl; add cold liquid and mix until smooth. As a rule, use 1 tablespoon of cornstarch to thicken every 2 cups of liquid to a medium consistency. After stirring the slurry into a cold liquid, bring it to a boil and simmer until the mixture thickens. Incorporate the slurry into whatever you are thickening.

Scallop Sauce

Ingredients:

10 oz scallops

3 tablespoons butter or margarine

½ cup chopped celery

6 green onions, with about 3 inches of green top, chopped

½ cup chopped carrots

1 to 1 ½ cups diced cooked ham

3 tablespoons flour

1 ¼ cups fish stock

¼-cup milk

1 ½ cups shredded low fat mozzarella and Cheddar cheese blend.

2 oz Sherry wine

Directions:

In a saucepan, melt butter over medium low heat; add celery, green onions, carrots, and ham. Sauté stirring frequently, until vegetables are tender. Add flour, stirring until well blended. Gradually add 1/4 cup milk, 1 1/4 cups fish stock, stirring constantly. Continue cooking, stirring constantly, until mixture is bubbly; add 1 cup cheese. Cook until cheese is melted; add more milk if mixture is too thick. Add sherry and stir.

Sautee scallops in oil or butter add to sauce.

Cook pasta noodles and drain. In baking dish add a layer of pasta then sauce, and then repeat layers. Bake at 325° for 45 minutes; top with remaining bake for about 10 minutes longer.

Spicy Sesame Dressing

Ingredients:

1 ½ teaspoons sesame seeds

1/3 cup reduced-sodium soy sauce

1/4 cup rice vinegar

1 tablespoon toasted sesame oil

½ clove garlic, minced

1 tablespoon light brown sugar

½ teaspoon chili-garlic sauce (see Ingredient Note)

¼ cup chopped scallions

Heat a small dry skillet over low heat. Add sesame seeds and stir constantly until golden and fragrant, about 2 minutes. Transfer to a small bowl and let cool.

Whisk soy sauce, vinegar, oil, garlic, sugar and chili-garlic sauce in another small bowl. Place in pan on stove and simmer until the sugar dissolves. Stir in scallions and the sesame seeds, cool and serve.

Five Mother Sauces + One

Velouté – Is a stock-based white sauce. It can be made from chicken, veal or fish stock. 3 tablespoons butter, 3 tablespoons flour, 2 cups chicken, fish, or veal stock, salt & white pepper. Melt butter in a saucepan over medium heat. Stir in flour and cook over medium, until mixture is smooth and bubbly, about 1 to 2 minutes. Slowly stir in stock. Heat to boiling, stirring constantly. Reduce heat to low, cook for 5 minutes, stirring occasionally. Salt and pepper.

Béchamel – Is a classic white sauce - a cream sauce. Stir milk into a butter-flour roux, the thickness of the sauce depends on the proportion of flour and butter to milk. The proportions for a thin sauce would be 1 tablespoon each of butter and 1 cup of flour per 1 cup of milk; a medium sauce would use 2 tablespoons each of butter and flour; a thick sauce, 3 tablespoons each. Use olive oil butter blend for healthier recipe.

Espagnole, or brown sauce, traditionally made of a rich meat stock, a mirepoix of browned vegetables (mix of diced onion, carrots and celery), a nicely browned roux, herbs and sometimes tomato paste. ½ bay leaf, 2 parsley stems, no leaves, 1/8 teaspoon dried thyme leaves, 1 clove garlic, 1 small onion, peeled, 1 carrot, peeled, 1 stalk celery, 1 clove garlic, 1/2 cup butter, 1/2 cup all-purpose flour, 2 tablespoons additional butter, 6 cups beef stock, 2 ounces tomato purée, 1/8 teaspoon salt and 1-1/8 teaspoon ground white pepper. .*Place the herbs and garlic in square of cheesecloth, called garni bag. Tie with string. Set aside. *Cut mirepoix. Set aside. Mince garlic. Heat the 1/2 cup butter in a small saucepan. Whisk in the flour to a paste consistency; cook over medium heat, stirring constantly, for 5 to 6 minutes until mixture (roux) bubbles, turns light brown in color. Set aside.

- Place the second half of butter in a heavy, 4-quart stockpot over medium heat. Add mirepoix. Sauté, stirring often, for about 5 to 6 minutes until it is well browned. Add minced garlic and sauté.

- Add roux to the vegetables, stirring to combine. Gradually, pour in the beef stock then the tomato purée.

- Add garni bag, dangle in the liquid. Boil, skimming off any impurities. Reduce heat and simmer, uncovered, for about 2 hours, skimming the surface, until the sauce is reduced to about 1 quart. Pour sauce and garni into a fine strainer lined with cheesecloth. Use a ladle or spoon to gently press any remaining vegetables through the strainer; toss out the rest. Salt and pepper.

Hollandaise sauce is made with an emulsion of egg yolks and fat. Hollandaise is made with clarified butter (140*), egg yolks and lemon juice salt pepper; whisk together quickly, adding butter slowly. Usually serve at room temperature. Toss out leftovers.

Vinaigrette sauce is made of a simple blend of oil, vinegar, salt and pepper (usually 3 parts oil to 1 part vinegar). Variations that are more elaborate can include any combination of spices, herbs, shallots, onions, mustard, etc.

Traditional vinaigrette is 1/4 cup red or white wine vinegar and 3/4 cup extra-virgin olive oil; add salt and ground pepper to taste. In a bowl whisk together the vinegar, salt, and pepper. Add olive oil in a small, slow stream to vinegar mixture and whisk until the mixture emulsifies. Taste and adjust seasoning as needed.

Tomato is considered the 6th of the 5 mother sauces.

1 small onion, cut into 1/4-inch dice, 4 cloves garlic minced, 3-ounces extra-virgin olive oil, 4 tablespoons fresh thyme, 2 (28-ounce) cans of tomatoes crushed and mixed well with their juices.

Sauté the onion and garlic in the olive oil over medium heat until translucent, but not brown - about 10 minutes. Add the thyme and cook 5 minutes more. Add the tomatoes. Bring to a boil, lower the heat to just bubbling, stirring occasionally for 30 minutes. Season with salt and pepper.

Fast and Easy Sauces

Garlic Sauce

2 tablespoons olive oil

2 tablespoon minced garlic (about ½ clove)

1 ½ tablespoons flour

1 tsp paprika

1-cup vegetable broth or chicken broth

1 teaspoon parsley

Salt pepper to taste

Heat oil on med low, add garlic 30 seconds to a minute (do not over brown), add flour, paprika and broth. Simmer 5 to 10 minutes.

Pesto

1-cup basil

1-cup pine nuts

½-cup olive oil

½-cup shredded parmesan

salt and pepper

Place all dry ingredients in blender; turn on low and add olive oil slowly.

Cocktail sauce

¼ c. low sodium ketchup

1 tablespoon lemon juice

    1 ½ prepared horseradish

    Mix and keep cold

Southwestern Beef Marinade

    1 large, garlic clove finely minced

    ¼ cup fresh lime juice

    ½ teaspoon ground cumin

    1 dash ground oregano

    2 tablespoons vegetable oil

    1 teaspoon kosher or coarse salt

    ¼ teaspoon freshly ground black pepper

Mix and keep at room temperature, place meat or vegetables in marinade and refrigerate for 1 hour and grill.

Little Naughty Sauces

Strawberry Mango Mint Sauce

    1 pint fresh strawberries clean and quartered

    1 fresh mango, pealed and diced

    1 bunch of chopped fresh mint

    1 jalapeño, seeded and finely diced

    1/3 cup finely diced red onion

    2 tablespoons strawberry jam.

    1 teaspoon apple cider vinaigrette

Mix all ingredients together; place in refrigerator 30 minutes.

    Great on fish

JALAPENO JAM

    1/3 cup blackberry jam

    1 jalapeños, diced and seeded

Mix. This is good at room temperature. *Excellent on Blackened fish

Cheddar Sauce

2-tablespoons butter

1-½ tablespoons flour

1-cup milk

½-cup shredded cheddar

1/3-cup parmesan cheese

½-tsp Dijon

¼-cup sherry wine

Salt pepper to taste

Melt butter, whip in flour; let it get nice and smooth (add a little more butter if not smooth). Gradually add milk, cheeses Dijon, thyme, salt and pepper. Let simmer 5 to 10 minutes.

Hot Fudge Sauce

1 c. sugar

1 ½ cup milk or water (still works)

2 tablespoon unsweetened cocoa

2 tablespoons light corn syrup

2 teaspoons butter

1 teaspoons salt

3 ounces bittersweet chocolate

1 tsp real vanilla

Add first six ingredients in saucepan; melt on medium heat, constantly stirring. Stir in vanilla and bittersweet chocolate until melted. Serve warm.

Yummy Yankee Pot Roast Stew

Ingredients:

1 (2 1/2 pound) boneless

bottom round roast

3 teaspoon salt and black ground pepper

2 onions, thinly sliced

3 cloves garlic, crushed

2 1/2 cups low sodium beef broth

1-cup water

1-cup red wine

3 teaspoons tomato paste

½ teaspoon crushed dried thyme

½ teaspoon crushed dried marjoram

2, russet potatoes, peeled and quartered

2 carrots, peeled, cut into two inch pieces

1 celery rib, coarsely chopped

Directions:

1. Season boneless bottom round roast with salt and pepper. Place meat in an oven broiler pan, broiling until brown on all sides.

2. Preheat oven to 450. Reduce oven temperature to 325°F.

3. In a heavy oven-safe deep pan, combine onions, garlic, beef broth, water, tomato paste, thyme, marjoram, and basil. Add roast and bring to a low

simmer. Cover tightly, return to oven, and cook for 1 1/2 hours.

4. Add potatoes, carrots, and celery; continue cooking for another hour.

5. Remove from oven; dice meat and dish into large bowls Take the onions, celery, and juice and heat until a soft boil and pour over roast.

White Chili Soup

Ingredients:

2 lbs cut up skinless chicken breast & skinless chicken thighs

¼-cup flour

7 each or 1-cup green chili fresh roasted – cleaned seeded and large dice

1 diced onion

1 coarse chopped garlic

2 diced tomatoes

1 ½ cup soaked navy bean

3-tablespoon chili powder

1 ½ tablespoon cumin

Salt & pepper to taste

1 ½ tablespoon onion powder

1 oz chicken base

1 oz beef base

Directions:

Wash and soak beans over night, then slow cook for one hour on stove or put in crock pot and cook four or five hours. Then cook chicken with flour and add to beans. Roast green chili and tomatoes under broiler, peel, seed and dice, then add to beans. Then season chili with chili powder, cumin, onion powder salt and pepper. Add chicken base and beef base. Let cook for one more hour or until beans are soft and meat is tender.

Pasta with Clam Sauce

Ingredients:

1 pound cooked pasta

2 cans minced clams, with juice

¼-cup butter

1/3 cup olive oil

½-cup fine diced shallots or red onions.

1/3 light half and half

½ teaspoon minced garlic

1 tablespoon dried parsley

Ground black pepper to taste

¼ tablespoon dried basil

¼-teaspoon thyme

3 oz white wine

3 oz dry sherry

Directions:

Sautee onions and garlic with olive oil until caramel color. Combine clams with juice, wine butter, parsley, basil, and pepper in a large saucepan. Place over medium heat until boiling. Add cooked pasta and sherry

Serve warm with fresh herbs as garnish.

Minestrone

Ingredients:

4 tablespoons extra virgin olive oil, divided

1 zucchini, cut into 1/2-inch dice & 1 yellow squash 1/2-inch dice

1 small carrot, finely diced (3/4 cup)

1 small onion, finely diced (1/2 cup)

2 cloves garlic, minced

1 teaspoon dried basil, thyme and oregano

1 32-ounce low sodium vegetable base or broth

1 8-ounce can tomato sauce

1 8-ounce can diced fire roasted tomatoes

1 15-ounce can canella beans, drained and rinsed low sodium

1/2 cup whole wheat blend elbow pasta

½-tablespoon fresh thyme

Salt and freshly ground black pepper

1/3 cup grated Parmesan cheese

1/3 cup Fresh basil, cut into strips.

Directions:

1. Heat the oil olive in large saucepan over medium-high heat. Add the zucchini, summer squash, carrot, onion, garlic and Italian seasoning and cook, stirring frequently, until the vegetables start to soften, about 10 minutes.

2. Stir in the base and tomatoes, cover, and bring to a boil. Add the beans, pasta and thyme and cook, uncovered, on low until the pasta is done, about 10 minutes. Add remaining olive oil and stir in.

3. Remove from heat and season with salt and pepper to taste. Top with the Parmesan cheese and basil. Do not over cook or pasta will get mushy.

Chapter 5: Salad & Dressings

Fruit Salad

  1 cup cantaloupe

  1 cup honeydew

  1 cup strawberries cut in quarters

  1 cup pealed kiwi

  1 cup grapes

  1 cup blueberries

  1 mango diced

Directions:

Dice all fruit, mix together and let set for 15 minutes so flavors come together.

Southwestern Caesar

Ingredients:

Add grilled chicken, shrimp or tofu for an entree salad.

2 small or 1 large head romaine lettuce, rinsed and blotted dry

6 oz corn tortillas

2 ears of fresh corn

3 red bell peppers

½ cup drained black beans

6 oz of diced tomatoes

1/2 cup grated cheddar cheese

Directions:

Place the corn, red and poblano peppers on a hot mesquite grill* - over hot coals, not high flames. Keep turning the vegetables so that they evenly char, without burning. Place peppers in a plastic bag, tie the top and let steam until cool enough to handle (about 15 minutes). Pull off the skin by hand. Remove stems, seeds and veins. Cut corn kernels off the cob.

Prepare dressing. Tear lettuce into bite-size pieces. Place the torn lettuce in a salad bowl. Add all ingredients except the dressing and tortilla strips. Add the dressing and toss to coat the greens. Portion salad on chilled plates and serve.

Garnish with protein and tortilla strips.

Serves 6

Southwestern Caesar Dressing

Ingredients:

3 large cloves garlic, chopped

2 anchovy fillets

3 large eggs (or 3 oz of pasteurized eggs)

½ cup red wine vinegar

2 tablespoons Dijon mustard

¼ cup fresh cilantro leaves

1 oz canned chipotle peppers in adobo sauce (caution hot)

½ teaspoon salt

½ teaspoon ground black pepper

½ cup grated Parmesan cheese

1 ½ cups olive oil

Combine all ingredients except the olive oil in a food processor and blend for 1 minute. Add olive oil slowly with the blender running.

3 corn tortillas cut into strips

½ teaspoon salt & ½ teaspoon white pepper

½ teaspoon chili powder

½ teaspoon cumin

Mix spices in a bowl set aside. Cut the corn tortillas into thin strips, drizzle oil, sprinkle dry spices over warm tortillas and bake in oven

Fancy Caprice Salad

Ingredients:

16 ounces fancy mixed greens

6 hot house tomatoes

4 ounces low sodium mozzarella cheese balls

8 leaves fresh basil chopped

3 teaspoons olive oil

4 ounces balsamic vinegar

Directions:

Dash of salt and cracked pepper

Sprinkle mozzarella, basil and tomatoes on top of salad.

Drizzle olive oil and balsamic over the tops and add a dash of salt and pepper, mix and serve.

Sheila Brillhart

BBQ Chicken Ranch Salad

Ingredients:

5 each crunchy breaded chicken breast strips, grilled chicken tenders, shrimp or tofu

3 oz of pre made BBQ Sauce

10 oz mixed baby greens

¼ cup roasted corn,

½ avocado diced

1 tablespoon black olives

3 oz toasted pine nuts

2 oz chopped green onions

1/3 cup low fat shredded cheddar and Monterey jack cheeses

2 oz light ranch dressing

Salt and pepper to taste

Directions:

Toss all fresh salad ingredients together. Chill. Cook off chicken strips in oven or on grill toss in BBQ sauce. Set aside. Toss ranch in tossed salad mix top with warm chicken, pine nuts, cheese and green onions.

Pear Candied Pecan Salad

Ingredients:

1 head leaf lettuce, torn into bite-size pieces

3 pears - peeled, cored and chopped

5 ounces blue cheese, crumbled

1 avocado - peeled, pitted, and diced

½ cup thinly sliced green onions

¼ cup white sugar

½-cup pecans

¼-cup olive oil

3 tablespoons red wine vinegar

1 ½ teaspoons white sugar

1 ½ teaspoons prepared mustard

1 clove garlic, chopped

½-teaspoon salt

Fresh ground black pepper to taste

Directions:

In a sauté pan over medium heat, stir 1/4 cup of sugar together with the pecans. Continue stirring gently until sugar has melted and the pecans are caramelized. Carefully place nuts onto waxed paper. Allow to cool, and break into pieces. Do not touch while cooking or cooling; candied nuts are extremely hot.

For the dressing, blend oil, vinegar, 1 1/2 teaspoons sugar, mustard, chopped garlic, salt, and pepper.

In a large serving bowl, place lettuce, pears, blue cheese, avocado, and green onions. Pour dressing over salad, sprinkle with pecans, and serve.

Wilted Spinach Salad

Ingredients:

10 to 12 ounces fresh spinach, washed, steamed and torn into bit-size pieces

¼ cup sliced red onion

2 hard-cooked eggs, 1 chopped, 1 sliced

2 to 4 slices bacon or turkey bacon, cooked crunchy

1 to 11/2 tablespoons bacon drippings

1 ½ tbsp. sugar

3 tbsp. vinegar

1 tbsp. water

½ tsp. salt

¼ tsp. pepper

Directions:

Place prepared spinach in a large bowl add onions. Refrigerate, tightly covered.

Fry or microwave bacon until crisp; remove to paper towel and set aside. In a small jar or measuring cup combine drippings with sugar, vinegar, water, salt and pepper. Refrigerate all ingredients until just before serving. When ready to serve, microwave the dressing on HIGH for 30 seconds, or until mixture boils.

Quickly toss the chopped egg with the greens, pour the hot dressing over greens mixture; toss again lightly. Top with sliced egg and crumbled bacon. Salt and pepper to taste.

For a healthy version, replace 1 tablespoon bacon drippings with liquid smoke and olive oil. Serves six.

Zesty Parmesan & Herb Vinaigrette

Ingredients:

Zesty Parmesan

(Awesome on arugula salads)

Ingredients:

2 tablespoons lemon juice

4 tablespoons olive oil

1/3 cup parmesan

Salt and cracked black pepper

Blend all ingredients except oil. While blender is running, add oil. Season vinaigrette with salt and pepper to taste.

Herb Vinaigrette

Ingredients:

1 tablespoon fresh chives

1 tablespoon fresh basil

¼ cup apple cider vinegar

1-teaspoon dijon mustard

½ shallot clean and chopped.

Blend all ingredients except oil. While machine is running add oil. Season vinaigrette with salt and pepper to taste.

Salmon Salciado Salad

Ingredients:

Salad

10 oz Fresh spinach, washed cleaned and dry.

5 oz mix of chopped green onions, tomato, snap peas, carrot, spinach and mango.

Divide green onions and tomatoes into to equal portions. Half for sautéing fish and half for salad.

Garnish 1 tablespoon toasted almonds, diced tomato and sliced green onions.

Sauce

2 tablespoons butter

2 tablespoons of soy

½ cup sherry wine

1/3 cup green onions

1/3 cup diced tomatoes

Direction:

Sauté salmon with butter, soy and sherry, turn heat down, turn fish over, add tomato and green onion and let sauce reduce; cook about 6 minutes. Set aside.

For service, mix tomato, green onion, snap peas, carrot, spinach and mango in a large bowl and chill. Then place salad mix in a large salad bowl, top with salmon and drizzle extra sauce over salad; garnish with toasted almonds, green onions, tomatoes and sauce reduction.

Chapter 6: Entrée's

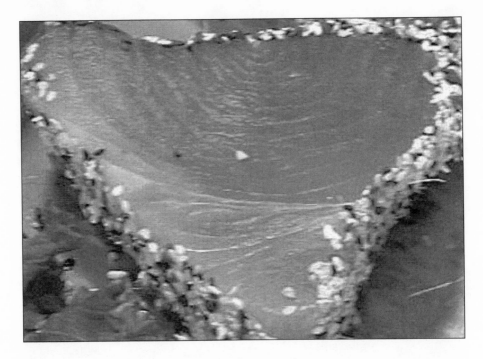

Encrusted Tuna

Ingredients:

1 loin of Sashimi Tuna

Mixture

1/2 cup black and white Sesame seeds

2 tablespoons Sea salt

1 tablespoon black pepper

2 tablespoons blend canola and olive oil.

Direction:

Coat tuna generously with mixture; heat oil, but do not let it smoke. Sear tuna on all sides about 11/2 to 2 minutes per side. This will cook rare to med-rare.

Sauce: Spicy sesame dressing (page 37)

Country Beef Potpie

Ingredients:

2 pounds stew beef, browned and drained

2 tablespoons all-purpose flour

1/4 cup olive oil

1 medium chopped peeled onion & 1 clove garlic, minced

3 1/2 cups water

2 ounces low sodium beef base

2 tablespoons Worcestershire sauce

1/4 teaspoon ground black pepper

1 1/2 cups diced potato

1 cup diced carrot

1 medium green bell pepper, seeded and chopped

1 (8-ounce) package frozen peas, thawed and drained

2 (9-inch) pie crusts

Direction: Preheat oven to 450°F.

1. Lightly coat beef with flour. Heat oil in a large, heavy skillet over medium-high heat until a drop of water sizzles in the oil; add beef and brown, stirring frequently, about 10 minutes; transfer to paper towels to drain. Return skillet to heat.
2. Add onion and garlic, sautéing until lightly browned, 4 to 6 minutes. Carefully stir in water, beef base or Beef bouillon cubes, salt, Worcestershire sauce and pepper. Return meat to skillet; reduce heat and simmer for about 1/2 hour.

81

3. Add potatoes, carrots and green pepper; simmer for another 20 minutes. Stir in peas at the end of cooking time.

4. Line a 9-inch pie pan with one of the crusts, letting the edge drape over the side; using a slotted spoon, fill pie with beef filling. Add a little of the cooking broth to filling, if desired. Top with remaining crust, fold bottom edge up over top edge; crimp edge with a fork and cut a few small slits in top crust to allow steam to escape while cooking.

5. Bake for 10 minutes: then reduce temperature to 350°F and bake for 30 more minutes.

Sweet Chicken Cordon Bleu and Horseradish Mashed Potatoes

Ingredients:

4 chicken breasts (single breasts, skinned & boned)

4 slices smoke ham

4 slices low sodium Swiss cheese

½ cup breadcrumbs

¼ cup plain flour

¼ cup honey mustard (you can make your own by using Dijon mustard and a little honey)

Directions:

One at a time, put the chicken breasts into a plastic bag, secure the top and pound them like crazy to flatten them out. Put one slice of smoked ham and one slice of Swiss cheese on each of the flattened chicken breasts.

Roll each chicken breast up with the smoked ham and cheese inside, then use a toothpick poked through to stop the parcel from unraveling. Roll each of the chicken breasts in the plain flour, then into the honey mustard, and finally in breadcrumbs.

Bake for approx 20 mines, or until you're sure the chicken is cooked all the way through until meat is a chalk white (165*) and the breadcrumbs are golden brown.

Horseradish Mashed potatoes

Ingredients:

1 ½ lbs Yukon gold potatoes, peeled and quartered

½ teaspoon salt pepper

4 tbsp 2% milk

2 tbsp butter

2 tbsp half and half

2 tbsp horseradish

Heat together. Add salt and pepper.

Directions:

Put potatoes into a saucepan. Add 1/2 teaspoon salt. Add water until potatoes are covered. Bring to boil, reduce heat and simmer, covered, 15-20 minutes, or until done - a fork can easily be poked through them. Warm milk and melt butter, together, either in microwave or in a pan on the stove. Drain water from potatoes. Put hot potatoes into a bowl. Add milk and melted butter. Use potato masher to mash potatoes. (Do not over-beat or your potatoes or they will get gluey.) Salt and pepper to taste.

Oven Fried Chicken Dinner

Ingredients:

2 pounds chicken, cut into pieces

1 cup plain/all purpose flour

2 teaspoons salt

1 teaspoon low sodium powdered chicken stock

1 teaspoon paprika

1 teaspoon pepper

2 tablespoons vegetable oil

Oven Fried Steak Fries

3 medium potatoes

1 tablespoon melted butter or mixture of equal parts butter and oil

3 tablespoons olive oil

1 teaspoon salt, 1/2 teaspoon pepper, or to taste, 1/4 teaspoon paprika, 1 teaspoon onion powder and1 teaspoon garlic powder.

Directions:

Rinse chicken pieces in cold water and pat them dry with some absorbent paper towel.

In a paper or plastic bag, combine the flour, paprika, salt, pepper and powdered chicken stock.

One piece at a time, put the chicken into the bag and shake it around to make sure that the chicken is completely coated in the flour & flavoring. Repeat the process for each of the chicken pieces. Heat the oil blend in sauté pan. When the oil has reached the desired temperature, brown on each side of the chicken in batches until the chicken is golden brown.

Drain each piece of chicken on some absorbent paper towel. Finish in the oven.

Oven Fries - Peel potatoes then cut crosswise into 3/8-inch slices. Brush with melted butter and oil. Bake at 425°, basting frequently with butter or butter mixture until tender and golden brown on both sides. Sprinkle with salt, pepper, onion powder and garlic powder.

Slow-Cooked Shredded Beef for Tacos

1 ½ pounds beef chuck roast

1 medium onion, sliced

1 cup water

1 Low sodium taco seasoning Mix

1 Diced Green Chiles

1 package taco shell or soft tortillas

Toppings: shredded lettuce, chopped tomato, shredded cheddar cheese, sour cream

Firehouse Salsa

1 med red onion diced, 2 each tomatoes diced, 1 can fire roasted tomatoes drained. 2 tablespoons V-8 Juice, 1/4 bunch cilantro chopped, 1 garlic clove chopped, 1 jalapeño seeded and diced. And 1 tablespoon olive oil

Leave chunky or blend in blender until thick; add more juice for thinner salsa.

Directions:

Place beef and onions in crock-pot

Combine water and seasoning mix in small bowl. Pour over beef and onion.

Cook on LOW for 6 to 8 hours or until tender.

Remove meat, shred beef with two forks.

Place beef in large bowl. Stir in a little base from crock-pot. Not to wet.

Fill warmed taco shells with beef mixture.

Top with lettuce, tomato, cheese, and sour cream and Firehouse salsa

Chicken Pomidori

Ingredients:

Chicken

2 boneless chicken breasts

1/2 cup panko bread crumbs

1/2 Tablespoon Italian seasoning

1/4 cup grated parmesan cheese, mozzarella blend

1 egg

3 tablespoons Olive oil

3 quarts water and one 12-ounce box whole wheat or durum semolina angel hair pasta

Sauce

3 vine-ripe tomatoes, coarsely chopped, 1 tablespoon minced garlic, 1 tablespoon red wine and balsamic vinegar, 1 tablespoon finely chopped fresh basil, 1/8 teaspoon black pepper, 1/4 teaspoon sea salt, optional, 1 tablespoon extra-virgin olive oil, 1 basil for garnish

Directions:

Boil Pasta off.. Flatten chicken to about 1/4 to 3/8 of an inch thick. In a shallow bowl, combine bread crumbs, Parmesan cheese and Italian seasoning. In another bowl, beat the egg. Dip chicken into egg, then coat with crumb mixture.

Use a spoon to coat chicken with the crumb mixture gently pressing crumbs onto chicken. Preheat a frying pan with about a 1/2 cup of olive oil. Add more when necessary.

Brown chicken on medium heat until nicely browned and juices run clear.

Sauce Mix all ingredients and simmer 10 to 15 minutes.

Serve pasta and sauce, lay chicken on top. Garnish with basil.

Sweet and Sour Chicken W/Rice Pilaf

Chicken

1 pound of chicken breast, skinless & boneless, sliced

Approx ½ pound pineapple pieces

2 cloves garlic, finely chopped & 2 onions, cut into large wedges

1 cucumber, de-seeded and cut into chunks

1 small bunch shallots, chopped

4 teaspoons sugar

4 teaspoons ketchup

2 tablespoons white vinegar

¼ teaspoon white pepper

2 teaspoons soy sauce

Olive oil blend for sautéing

Rice Pilaf

1 cup water hot 1-teaspoon chicken stock

1 cup sliced fresh mushrooms

¾ cup rice (instant)

½ cup shredded carrot

¼ teaspoon dried marjoram

¼ cup thinly sliced green onions

¼ cup green bell pepper diced

1 tablespoon cut fresh parsley pinch of fresh ground pepper

½ teaspoon ground garlic

Directions:

Chicken - In a large frying pan, heat oil and add chicken and garlic.

Cook - stirring continuously - for 5 minutes, or until the chicken is cooked.

Add in onion, and pineapple; cook for 3 minutes, or until the onion has softened.

Add soy sauce, sugar, vinegar, tomato sauce/ ketchup & pepper.

Cook - stirring continuously for 1 minute.

Add salt just prior to serving.

Serve on a bed of steamed brown rice or jasmine rice.

Rice - In a medium saucepan, stir together water and dry chicken bouillon. Bring to a boil. Stir in the fresh cut mushrooms and peppers, uncooked brown rice, carrots, marjoram, and black pepper. Return to a boil; reduce heat to a low simmer; cover and simmer cook for 12 minutes more. Remove from heat and let steam cook for 5 minutes. Fold or stir in the green onions and parsley.

Tip: Brown rice will take a lot more time to cook

Shrimp Creole or Shrimp Scampi

Shrimp Scampi Ingredients:

½ pounds large shrimp (26-30) peeled and divined

2 teaspoons olive oil and 1 teaspoon butter

2 tablespoons minced garlic

¼ teaspoon paprika

¼ teaspoon black pepper

¼ cup bottled clam juice

1 tablespoon lemon juice

2 tablespoons minced fresh parsley or 2 teaspoons dried

Directions:

Heat oil and butter in a large non-stick skillet over medium high heat; then add garlic and sauté for 1 minute, stirring constantly. Add shrimp and cook, stirring until shrimp are firm and pink, about 3 to 4 minutes. Do not overcook. Add paprika, clam juice and lemon juice. Boil until half of the liquid is evaporated. Remove from heat and stir in parsley.

Shrimp Creole

½ cup diced celery & 1 ¼ cups chopped onion

¾ cup chopped bell pepper

1 (8 ounce) can tomato sauce & 1 (28 ounce) can diced tomatoes and 1 clove garlic

1 teaspoon salt & ¼ teaspoon pepper

2 teaspoons Tabasco sauce (optional)

1 cup uncooked long grain rice

1 pound shrimp, cleaned and shelled

1 teaspoon garlic salt or ¼ teaspoon garlic powder

Combine all ingredients except shrimp. Cook for 1 1/2 to 2 1/2 hours in crock pot on HIGH or for 4 to 5 hours in crock pot on LOW. Add shrimp for the last hour of cooking. Or cook on stove for 45 minutes to an hour or until sauce has evaporated and rice is cooked.

Succulent Salmon Burger

Ingredients:

　　1 12 oz can salmon

　　1 egg

　　½ cup corn flake crumbs

　　¼ cup chopped onions

　　¼ cup uncooked oatmeal

　　2 tablespoons lemon juice

　　2 tablespoons mayonnaise

　　2 tablespoons Dijon

　　1 teaspoon bay seasoning

　　1 teaspoon dried dill

　　2 tablespoons black and white sesame seeds

Directions:

Mix well. Make into four large or six small patties. Grill over a finely meshed grill screen on the barbecue grill or broil far away from the heat in a broiler for about six minutes on each side.

　　Coleslaw goes nicely with this.

Yummy Drummies

Ingredients:

2 ½-cup water

3 lbs. chicken drummies or drumsticks.

1 ¼ cup barbecue sauce

1 teaspoon liquid smoke

2 Tablespoon chili sauce

¼ cup honey

3 cloves garlic, minced and dash of salt and pepper

1 bay leaf

Directions:

Pat the chicken drummies dry with a paper towel and place on broiler pan. Broil 5-6 inches from the heat for 8-10 minutes, turning often, until chicken is browned. Place in 3-4 quart crock-pot. Mix remaining ingredients in a small bowl and pour over drummies. Cover and cook on LOW for 4-5 hours.

For crisp place back on broiler pan, place under broiler about 5 to 8 minutes

These can be held for 1 hour after the cooking time on LOW. Toss in sauce

Honey BBQ or BBQ Franks Hot sauce

Vegetarian Red Beans and Rice

Ingredients:

2 cups cold water

1 cup dried kidney beans

2 tablespoons butter

1 medium onion chopped

1 medium green pepper chopped

1 cup uncooked long grain rice

1 teaspoon salt

3 teaspoons Cajun spice

Directions:

Beans bring beans to a boil in a large saucepan. Boil for 2 minutes then remove from heat cover and let stand for 1 hour. Return the beans to range. Add water to cover beans if necessary. Heat to a boil, reduce heat fast to a very low simmer, cover and cook until tender. 1 to 1 ½ hours. Drain beans reserving liquid.

Rice

Melt butter, stir in onions, garlic, rice. Add green peppers. Stir until onions are tender but still crispy. Add 2 cups of bean liquid to onions, green peppers and rice and Cajun spice and salt to beans in a 3 quart sauce pan. Heats to a boil, stirring rarely, reduce heat to simmer cover and let cook 14-15 minutes. Remove from heat fluff and let steam covered 5 minutes. Pour beans over rice.

Sautéed Spinach and Crazy Good Asparagus

Sautéed Spinach

Ingredients:

10 oz fresh spinach, washed

1/2 med onion, diced

3 tablespoons olive oil

1 tablespoon minced garlic

1 tablespoon balsamic

Directions:

Wash spinach and slice onion. Place oil in wok or sauté pan, heat to smoking point. Add onion to wok, stir. Add spinach and garlic, stir spinach from bottom to top add balsamic. Cover wok briefly. Lift cover up and keep stirring spinach until it is wilted. Cook the spinach a full five minutes, covering and uncovering the wok as you are stir frying. Season with salt and pepper

Crazy Good Asparagus

1 pound asparagus

1/3 cup Italian salad dressing

1/3 cup balsamic dressing.

1 tablespoon minced garlic

1 tablespoon Worcestershire sauce

Salt and pepper

Cut one inch off the bottom of the asparagus. Wash. In a shallow 9 inch casserole dish, place the asparagus in the dish and cover with the above marinade. Let sit one to three hours.

Prepare the grill for the direct heat method. Grill the asparagus using a medium-hot temperature and baste with the marinade frequently. Grill for no more then six minutes.

Nice Green Beans

Green Beans

Ingredients:

2 tablespoons extra-virgin olive oil

3 medium red onions (about 1 3/4 pounds), cut into 16 wedges each

1 pound green beans, trimmed

1/2 cup vegetable broth

1 tablespoon balsamic vinegar

1 tablespoon apple cider vinegar

2 teaspoons light brown sugar

1/4 teaspoon salt

½ teaspoon powder ginger

Salt and freshly ground pepper to taste

Directions:

Heat oil in a large skillet over medium heat add onions and cook, stirring occasionally, until golden.

Meanwhile, bring a large saucepan of lightly salted water to a boil. Add green beans and cook, uncovered, until crisp-tender, 5 to 10 minutes. Drain.

Add broth and beans to the onions; cook for 5 minutes. Stir in vinegars, brown sugar, ginger, salt and pepper. Cover and cook for 2 minutes. Serve warm

Calabacitas Con Queso

Ingredients:

1 ½ lb zucchini, unpeeled -- cut in 1/4 " cubes

1 cup water

Salt and pepper

2 tablespoons olive oil

1 large garlic clove

1 cup finely chopped onion

¾ cup diced red bell peppers

2 cups corn kernels

1 tablespoon chili powder

1 teaspoon cumin

2 green chili peppers, roasted, peeled and chopped

Garnish with ½ lb shredded Monterey jack cheese

Directions:

Mix approximations: 5 to 6 zucchini; 1 medium onion; 1 large or 2 small red peppers; 10-ounce bag of corn, or 16-ounce can. Place diced zucchini in medium saucepan with water, season lightly with salt and pepper. Bring to a boil and simmer, covered, over medium heat until slightly tender but still crunchy, about 2 minutes. Set aside without draining.

Heat oil in large skillet until hot, but not smoking. Reduce heat slightly; add garlic, red bell peppers, and onion and cook, stirring, until onion is translucent, about 2 minutes. Cook until liquid partly evaporates, about 5 minutes. Stir in corn and green chili and simmer 5 minutes.

BBQ Beef Brisket in the Oven

Ingredients:

1 whole brisket

½ cup chili powder

½ cup salt

¼ cup granulated garlic

¼ cup granulated onion

¼ cup ground black pepper

2 tablespoons dry mustard

2 bay leaves

1 cup beef base

8 oz water or red wine

Direction:

1. Combine all ingredients, except beef broth and brisket, and mix well.

2. Season brisket on both sides with mixture, and place in a pan

3. Roast in a preheated 350°F oven for 1 hour.

4. Combine beef broth with equal amount of water. Add enough liquid to the roasting pan to achieve 1/2-inch liquid in pan. Cover roasting pan, lower heat to 325°F and continue to roast for 4 to 5 hours, basting frequently. You can substitute 1 cup red wine for water.

5. Pull from oven when thermometer reaches 145°F. Let rest 15 minutes before slicing.

6. Trim fat, slice meat thinly across the grain.

Chapter 7: Sweet Treats

Berry Bowl

Ingredients:

1 cup blueberries

1 cup raspberries

½ cup strawberries

1 tablespoon orange juice

1 teaspoon maple syrup

1 tablespoon fresh chopped mint

1 teaspoon fresh chopped basil

Directions:

In large bowl, toss raspberries, blueberries and strawberries. In a small bowl, mix all dressing ingredients until smooth. Serve fruit with dressing

Fresh berries can be used in desserts or savory dishes, eaten out of hand, dried, or made into delicious jams, jellies, or preserves to keep or give as gifts. Blueberries, strawberries, and blackberries are among the most popular berries

Big Berry Smoothie

Ingredients:

1 ½-cup blueberries

1 ½-cup strawberries

1 cup mixed berry juice

¼ cup low fat vanilla yogurt

1 teaspoon chopped mint

4 each ice cubes

1 teaspoon honey

Serves 2

Directions: Combine all ingredients in blender until smooth.

Passion Smoothie

Ingredients:

1 ½ cup frozen passion fruits

1 ½ cup strawberries

1 banana

1-cup orange juice

1/3 low fat vanilla yogurt

1-teaspoon honey

Serves 2

Directions: Combine all ingredients in blender until smooth.

Pomegranate-Pear

Ingredients:

½ cup blueberries

½ cup fresh pears

1 ½-cup pomegranate juice

1 cup orange juice

3 each ice cubes

Serves 2

Directions: Combine all ingredients in blender until smooth

Cranberry Crave

Ingredients:

1 ½-cup blueberries

½ cup strawberries

1-teaspoon fresh basil

1/3 cup low fat vanilla yogurt

1 ½ cup cranberry juice

4 each ice cubes

1 teaspoon honey

Serves 2

Directions: Combine all ingredients in blender until smooth

Deep Chocolate Mocha Cake

Ingredients:

1 container (8 ounces) light sour cream

½ cup cooled freshly-brewed coffee

½ teaspoon vanilla

2 squares unsweetened chocolate

½ cup (1 stick) butter

1 ½ cups sugar

2 eggs

1 ½ cups flour, divided

1 teaspoon each baking soda and ground cinnamon

½ teaspoon each baking powder and salt

Directions:

Mix dry ingredients; set aside. Mix everything else except butter and unsweetened chocolate. Melt butter on low heat. Add chocolate; incorporate to wet ingredients and mix. Slowly add dry ingredients to wet. After everything is incorporated, grease an 8x8 square pan and pour batter. Let cook at 350° for 35 minutes

Dusting:

Mix 2 teaspoons unsweetened cocoa, 2 teaspoons powder sugar. and 1 teaspoons cinnamon or hot fudge sauce on page 39.

Big Treat Dark Chocolate Snicker Cookies

Ingredients:

2 ½ cups all-purpose flour

1 teaspoon salt

2 teaspoon baking soda

¼ cup unsweetened coco powder

2 cups *I Can't Believe It's Not Butter*, softened

1 ½ cups packed brown sugar

½ cup white sugar

2 eggs

2 teaspoons vanilla extract

½ large bag of semisweet chocolate chips

2 Snicker Bars, chopped in food processor

Directions:

1. Preheat oven to 350° F (175° C). Sift together salt, coco powder, flour and baking soda, set aside.

2. In a large bowl, cream together the butter, brown sugar, and white sugar. Beat in the instant pudding mix until blended. Stir in the eggs and vanilla. Blend in the flour mixture. Finally, stir in the chocolate chips and Snickers. Drop cookies by rounded spoonfuls onto lightly spread un-greased cookie sheets.

3. Bake for 10 to 12 minutes in the preheated oven. Edges should be golden brown.

Crumbly Coffee Cake

Ingredients

1 box low sugar yellow or white cake mix

1 box- fat free Instant vanilla pudding

2/3 cup salad oil

2 eggs

1/2 cup water

1 teaspoon vanilla

2 teaspoons cinnamon; separate in two halves

2 teaspoons unsweetened cocoa; separate in two halves

1 cup granulated sugar; separate in two halves.

Direction:

Beat cake mix, vanilla pudding mix, oil, egg and water. Pour into greased dish (9 x 13) or 8 inch round pans.

Mix cocoa, cinnamon, granulated sugar, (nuts or raisins if desired). Sprinkle over batter and marbleizes through with a knife. Bake at 355° for 35-45 minutes. Cake has tendency to fall as it cools.

To make topping in a small bowl, mix together sugar, flour and cinnamon. Cut in margarine with fork, place half over batter and swirl. Spoon remaining topping over batter and sprinkle with nuts. Bake for an additional 30 minutes.

Sweet Pecan Apple Cake

Ingredients:

¾ cup raw sugar

¼ cup butter

1 egg

1 teaspoon cinnamon

1 teaspoon baking soda

1 tablespoon vanilla

1¼-cup flour

2 cups chopped, pealed red apples

¼ chopped pecans

Directions: Pre heat oven to 350°

Mix sugar and butter. Add egg and beat. Gradually add remaining ingredients. Mix well. Pour batter into 8x8x2 pan. Bake for 30 minutes.

Glaze

1 cup sugar

1 teaspoon cinnamon

½ teaspoon nutmeg

¼ teaspoon salt

½ cup apple juice

½ cup water

Combine all ingredients and simmer on low 2 to 3 minutes. Finish with a tablespoon butter melted in sauce off stove. Cool and glaze.

Cinnamon Rolls

Ingredients:

1 ½ packages (about 3-1/4 teaspoons) dry yeast

¼-cup warm water

½ cup shortening

¼ cup sugar

1 ½ teaspoon salt

1 cup milk

1 egg

4 to 5 cups sifted flour

½ cup melted butter

½ cup brown sugar

2 tablespoons cinnamon

½ cup raisins (optional)

Vanilla Frosting

2 cups powdered sugar

1 tablespoon butter, melted

1 teaspoon vanilla

2 to 4 tablespoons milk or cream

Pre-made frosting works as well

Directions:

Add the warm water to the yeast and soak 10 minutes.

Scald milk; pour over the shortening. Add sugar and salt and cool. Add the dissolved yeast to flour mix until dough forms. Turn dough into well-oiled bowl. Let rise for 11/2 hours. Press dough down. Dough should be soft yet firm enough to handle. Knead on floured board; if still sticky, add a little more flour.

Divide into workable size. Roll dough out into a rectangle. Cover with melted butter. Layer with a generous thick layer of brown sugar and cinnamon. If you like raisins, layer on a layer of raisins. Roll up jellyroll fashion.

Slice with either dental floss or sharp knife, about 1 to 1-1/2 inches thick. Place slices in an 11x9 inch greased pan. Place in rows with about 1/2 inch in between. Let rolls rise until they fill the pan generously...about another hour.

Bake rolls at 350° for 20 to 25 minutes; check to see if golden brown; if not, cook additional 5 to 10 minutes. Check often.

Cool and frost.

Chewy Chocolate Chips

Ingredients:

1 ½ cups all-purpose flour

2 teaspoon baking soda

2 cups butter, softened

1 ½ cups packed brown sugar

½ cup white sugar

1 packages instant low fat –low sugar vanilla pudding mix

4 eggs

2 teaspoons vanilla extract

1 large bag of semisweet chocolate chips

2 cups chopped pecans

Directions:

1. Preheat oven to 350° F (175° C). Sift together the flour and baking soda; set aside.

2. In a large bowl, cream together the butter, brown sugar, and white sugar. Mix in the instant pudding. Stir in the eggs and vanilla. Mix in the flour mixture. Finally, stir in the chocolate chips and nuts. Drop cookies by rounded spoonfuls onto lightly spread greased cookie sheets.

3. Bake for 10 to 12 minutes in the preheated oven. Edges should be golden brown. For chewier cookies, cook 8 to 10 minutes.

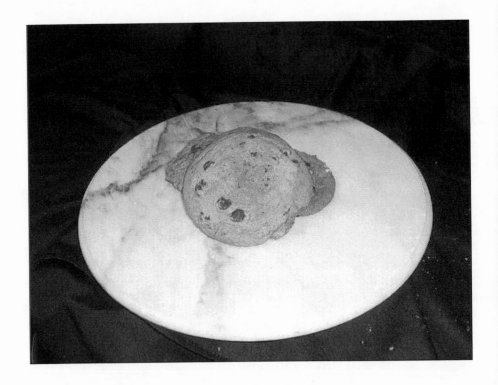

ACKNOWLEDGMENTS

To Tommy who has fought the fight with me. I know the courage it has taken to stand by me when you have wanted to run away. I do know you too have been a casualty of this disease. Thank you for being my happy taster for all the different foods that have made this book possible. To say I love you is an understatement.

To my parents and family, who have cheered me on and have encouraged me to fight and cook at each obstacle and to have gratitude for each new day. I do know you are only a phone call away, always my eternal safety nets. Thank you sincerely. I love you all so much.

To my dearest friend Dana: your kindness and humor is stronger than any medicine, you have shown me that with courage and a little humor anything is possible. You talked until I listened, what more could I ask for. Thank you.

To my sweet dear friend Sally: your insight, encouragement and awesome ability to see to the heart of the matter made this cookbook a pleasure to write. For you, my friend, for this and a million other little reasons I am forever in your debt. In addition, of course, thank you for trusting me to be the chef for your VIP Christmas parties.

Jocelyn, what can I say. You make me laugh. You may not be blood but you have stood by me as if you are. Thank you.

Eat Well...

The Intensity of Chef Sheila's life is matched only by the intensity of her cooking.

Chef Sheila's very personal battle with asthma and corticosteroids has produced a book that combines sound nutritional advice with delicious healthy recipes of interest to anyone on corticosteroids.

Sally Wenzel

Made in the USA
San Bernardino, CA
07 December 2012